What people
How I bough

"I've known Freddie as a friend and fellow business owner for years. And when he told me a few years ago that he was going to build a profitable property portfolio in just 12 months, I didn't really believe him. Freddie's a clever chap, but who could do that in the worst property recession in living memory?

And yet he did it! This book documents his journey so that you can avoid his mistakes and benefit from the shortcuts he learned.

Freddie is not one of those property gurus you hear about. He's an ordinary person with a genuine motivation to increase his income levels quickly, who has used property to do it. This will change the way you think about building your asset base and increasing your personal income"

Paul Green ~ Growth UK

"Freddie's book is a real eye opener, really down to earth and full of genuine case histories of what to do, and importantly what not to to whilst building a property portfolio in such a short time frame, particularly if you want to use the same strategies that enabled Freddie to buy houses for just one pound!

This is a typical example of the 'just do it' principle, exactly what I recommend to all our NABO clients.

Jonathan Jay ~ Founder of NABO *The National Association Of Business Owners*

How I bought a House for a £1

Freddie Rayner

How I bought a house for a £1

Copyright 2013 © Freddie Rayner

www.FreddieRayner.com

ISBN 978-1-907308-30-7

First published in Great Britain by Compass Publishing

Set and designed by The Book Refinery Ltd

Freddie Rayner asserts the rights to be identified as the author of this work.

Contents

Introduction

I started out on my journey as a 64 year old ex-cleaner determined to find a way to earn more money.

A lot more money!

I convinced myself that I needed to earn an extra £50,000 per year, in the shortest time I could, part time.

I gave myself one year in which to do it as by then I would be collecting my old age pension.

I didn't know the rules, so I just carried on and made it happen.

I found a way to earn my target amount but couldn't do it in one year, but my success brought me enough experience to easily go on to achieve *much bigger* financial goals.

I now know how to help people with property problems, and help them overcome them. I discovered that another group of people desperately needed to own their own homes and couldn't because of all sorts of impositions imposed on them, and I discovered that I could help these people to realise their dream of home ownership, in so doing I now found myself in a better position to help me achieve my personal financial goals.

I sincerely hope that I can help you achieve your personal goals too.

This is a record of my first year.

Okay, so right from the off, I am not super intelligent, it's not my style, and I'm just not clever enough. For academic achievement I got one O level, and that was for truancy!

For years, I was a cleaner – a door-to-door cleaner. I knocked on doors; a short few words to find out if the person living there wanted something cleaned; a carpet or a three-piece suite, oven or even the whole house from top to bottom. I was your man – *nothing clever about that.*

On 4th January 1997, my wife told me that she was going to see the doctor before she went to work. She worked as a P.A. to the Finance Director of Travis Perkins, the builder's merchant whose head office is in Northampton, where we both live. I didn't enquire as to why as I thought it must be a 'women's issue' or something like that.

I went off in my van to Silverstone Village, to knock on doors and do some cleaning or whatever. When I got home, around 6.00 pm, no one was in, which was a bit strange. So I phoned one of Ruth's friends from work to find out if they knew where she was. I was told that she did not turn up that day, *even more strange!*

I then called the out-of-hours doctor's surgery, only to discover that my wife had had an 'incident,' and had been admitted to the General Hospital.

I then went off to the hospital where I discovered that my wife had died in the doctor's surgery, been resuscitated, then the paramedic arrived, who also gave her resuscitation after she died again, then she was rushed off to the hospital and was now in Intensive Care!

I was met by a nurse and doctor who informed me that Ruth probably wouldn't make it through the night, and I was to prepare for the worst.

Well, the upshot was that Ruth had had a cardiac arrest

in the doctor's surgery, died twice technically, was resuscitated and then lived.

The next day she was still alive!

She went on to have a defibrillator fitted (much the same as the footballer, Fabrice Muamba did just recently). She did, however, have a *long road* to recovery. As the doctors were unsure of why Ruth's heart had just given out, she had to go for test after test, all in Oxford, a 90-mile round trip. Some of the tests took 15 to 20 minutes, and some a whole day. This went on for months, every other day, and for me working as a self-employed cleaner, with no work, and no pay, <u>we were running on empty.</u>

I got some work via the Oxford Borough Council, as I was there so often, doing the sort of jobs you see on programmes like 'Life of Grime'.

Yuk! *I hated each and every job.*

Stinky, vile jobs that made me wish I was able to do something else! I only ever did five of those jobs and I made more money than I would normally make by a factor of around five. Nevertheless, I disliked each and every day, and Ruth was making progress and recovering. I wrote on a piece of paper *"Any day above ground is a good day,"* and we've kept it to this day.

Halfway between Oxford and Northampton is Milton Keynes, well positioned in case I had to stop everything and rush off to the Oxford hospital should Ruth need attention, I then tried to get work from Estate Agents in Milton Keynes doing cleaning for end of lets etc., and they gave me jobs a-plenty!

All clean jobs (anything could be considered a clean job

after what I had been **through in Oxford)!**

The trouble was as I **discovered, hardly** *anyone* ever paid on time. This meant that **I was always working,** always invoicing, but then I was *always broke!*

I could not see a way out. **Then I got a big contract to do** all the cleaning for a **nurse's home in a well-known** hospital. I did the work; **six weeks, all on my own, working** 12 hours a day, six days **a week, but the contractor went** bust and I *never* got paid!

This was a blow that **I thought I would** *never recover from.* I literally started out **flat broke, only to find that 18** months later I was **much worse off!**

I had a 'poor old me' moment **that lasted around three** days, where I was too drunk to **care. Ruth thought I'd lost** the plot, and I thought I'd **hit rock bottom. When I** sobered up, I thought to myself, **sod it!** I'm a cleaner, that's my lot in life. So I'll be a *great cleaner,* and I'll clean private houses only, at a really **attractive hourly rate!**

I then got some leaflets printed **(paid for by my mother-** in-law) and put them out **door-to-door in Towcester. (I** explain in section 4 how to **use these effectively)**

It worked!

Four clients, then 10 clients, **then 100 clients, and so on** until we got to 300 clients, **all of whom paid on time, and** I didn't do any of the cleaning!

What I did do here quite literally changed my fortunes forever, but it took a long while for me to understand the implications of what I was about to implement.

This is where I got the client to pay me in advance!

WOW!

What a revelation!

And what a boost to my then meagre income, this was the start of a whole new chapter in our lives, and I never even knew it. When we had got to 300 clients, Ruth said, *"Why don't we franchise this idea?"* So, we got ourselves a Franchise Consultant, and well, that worked too, and now this cleaner and his wife had a business to be proud of, and we still are to this day.

We had been running our cleaning business for many years quite successfully; we were reasonably well off, but not rich. I wasn't complaining; we liked our life. We liked most of our franchisees and most of them liked us.

It was a nice life.

Ruth's mum had a stroke and ended up in a care home because her dad couldn't cope with Ruth's mum at home. Then he got Alzheimer's, had a heart attack and also ended up in the same care home, the cost of which was considerable because Ruth wanted them to be together for whatever time they had left. It was expensive; the home that they owned outright had to be sold, the pension Ruth's dad received after 25 years in the Police, some of which was as an armed Royal Protection Officer and earned him a £20k per year was also taken, plus their savings of £20k, all their old age pensions too. *Everything they had, in fact.*

I worked out that we would need <u>one million pounds plus,</u> in ready cash to pay the care home payments for 10 years for them, or us if we too needed putting in care.

This was the catalyst for change.

I needed more money than I thought. I needed more money than *anyone* thought, after all, it wouldn't be me that needed care, nor Ruth, it happens to other people, right?

Wrong!

It was happening <u>to us</u>. We were told that after the money ran out, *we* would need to TOP UP the funds for them to stay in this home, at a cost of around <u>£1500 per week</u>!

I started my search for how to make extra money. I looked into this; I looked into that, spent a small fortune discovering how to become a millionaire on the Internet, only to discover it would never be for me, or other daft ideas that looked good until I had spent my money only to discover, yet again, *that I'd been had.*

Then I read a book called *'Rich Dad Poor Dad'* by Robert Kywasiki.

WOW!

What a revelation!

I started to investigate the world of property, *but a word of warning*; I did not know what shark bait looked like until I ventured into this world!

I looked in the mirror one day and saw *'shark bait'* written all over me.

Some of the 'Property Gurus', you know the ones, *"I earn £40 million from 250 properties before breakfast,"* type of people, they do earn a fortune, from shark bait like me or you, <u>so please be warned</u>!

On a brighter note, there are also some good guys too –

just do your research properly.

Anyway, I got started in property and after just one year I had acquired nine properties, and that monetised at **£35,400 per year**, all of it on a <u>part-time basis</u>. To make more money, I needed to do much the same for the second and subsequent years but leaving out all the stupid mistakes I'd made in the first year.

When I talk to other property novices like me, they ask me what I did that was wrong, what did I learn from each one, how could it have been done differently and how could they benefit from my learning curve?

Luckily for me, *I recorded each acquisition*, and I'm going to **share each one of them with you.** I am going to <u>show you</u> how you too can follow my lead in your local area, and *earn much the same* extra income, over and above what you are earning right now, *and* on a part-time basis!

Jargon you might not be familar with

Throughout this book, I will be referring to certain phrases that are all part of the house buying process. If you see an asterisk (*) beside the phrase, then the explanation is at the end of that chapter.

However, there are also many phrases that I use that are specific terms. These I have added to the Glossary on page 112. It's important that you understand what all these phrases mean, so make sure you fully understand them before you start.

Section 1

Foundations for Success

Do You Have a Pension?

I don't, I never got around to it. It doesn't matter to me now, but if I had had a pension, I *bet* you it would not be worth the figure that it would have promised me when I took it out – Gordon Brown saw to that didn't he?

Property is a great vehicle to providing a *secure* pension pot.

In the past 15 years, annuity rates have fallen by some 45%. In contrast, the average house price has *risen* by over 260% *despite* the recent credit crunch. The average pension pot is £30,000 for a man aged 65. This would have meant an annuity worth £3,300 a year in 1995, compared with only £1,800 a year today, and to cap that the state pension, given the state of the country's finances, will *not even exist* in its present form by the time most of you reading this will need it. So, what are you going to do about it?

Doing nothing is <u>NOT</u> an option!

So, *where* do you start?

What do you buy?

How can you buy?

Should you choose your own locality, further afield, or even overseas? Do you need a limited company? How much money (if any) will you need? Should you manage the properties yourself or use a letting agency? Will you make enough money? Will you lose all your money? Along with many, many more questions yet to be answered.

You mustn't fall into the trap of deciding on which to

choose, or where, or even if! These are just details that can stop you from the action you need to take to get going. You can decide *later* all the whats and wheres.

I have been too far too many property-related meetings, where when I meet up with other delegates and ask how they are doing, *all* seem to say the same things like, *"I'm looking for the right area", "I'm thinking about my upside/downside (whatever that means),"* or all sorts of **excuses** as to why they haven't done anything at all, except confuse themselves totally!

Research is *one* thing, but confusion stems from *over analysing*, and that leads to procrastination, which means <u>nothing gets going.</u>

It all boils down to fear of the unknown. We all recognise that fear is good, up to a point, it's a natural instinct, but we must learn to control it and do something.

> *"A journey of one million miles begins with a single step." ~ **Confucius***

Well, congratulations!

You've already taken your first step by *reading this book*!

What You Will Learn

Within this book, there's enough information for anyone to get started on the exciting journey of property for profit.

Use it as a guide to the next steps required. *Use the knowledge of others* that are already ahead of you in the game. It's a bit like being in a minefield; one false move and you could be blown up! But someone has already made it across safely, and luckily they left their footprints in the mud all the way over to the other side! **Will you follow them?** If your answer is *no* or *maybe*, then property probably isn't for you just yet.

When starting out in any new venture, the fear of failure is bound to be uppermost in your thoughts. Everyone reading this book is starting off from different points of in terms of life experience, relationships, finances and education etc., so the fear of failure will be interpreted differently from person to person.

But what's the worst that can happen?

People don't get hanged anymore; you won't get sent to prison (unless you really do something totally stupid).

Could you lose some money? Could you lose 'face' (i.e. die of embarrassment)? Could you get over it? *Yes, of course you could!* If you bought a pigsty of a property at auction and potentially were set to lose money, you could always put it up for auction again, *lesson learnt!*

Something I learned a long time ago was;

> *"If you think education is expensive, try ignorance." ~ **Derek Bok***

You don't, however, need to <u>over</u>-educate yourself; you probably need to learn to just take baby steps first. Get a couple of properties, make some money, buy some more, and make more money, until you achieve your own personal goals.

The first part is, of course, going to be the hardest, but

that's just because it will all be new to you, as it was to me.

They say, *"Hindsight is a wonderful thing."* Just imagine if you'd bought properties 20 years ago, rented them out, and had the tenants pay your mortgage off for you.

How would that make you feel? Well, here we are in 2013 with property set at the lowest levels since the 2007 property price crash. Would you like to be able to buy property right now? How many properties would you buy? In this book, I'll tell you how many properties I've bought and *regretted*, and how many I've bought and felt amazing about afterwards (particularly as four of them cost me £1 each!).

There are thousands more to be had out there, so don't let fear paralyse you into doing nothing; try not to over analyse what might happen, *just get out there and do it.*

Waiting for the right property, the right location, or the lowest rate of mortgage product will hamper your success before you even get started – **you really have to commit to action.** All of us (me included) have our comfort zones, and you need to be prepared to *step out of yours and try new things to help you overcome the fear of the unknown.* You'll soon realise that fear is simply an illusion.

My biggest fear was the fear of failure. I didn't want to be seen as the biggest idiot around for making ludicrous claims about being a property guy, (starting out as I did aged 64 and being an ex-Cleaner), but I told everyone that I would get properties under my belt and improve my lot in life, or die trying. *Well, I didn't die, and I certainly tried!*

As I write I have nine properties under my control, and as Donald Trump has often been quoted, *"Own nothing, control everything"*. So if it's good enough for Donald Trump, billionaire businessman, it's good enough for me.

I didn't know it when I started, but my reason for starting in the property business, was financial gain for myself. Nothing wrong with that, but as I've progressed I've seen things I would never have imagined.

Many homeowners have suffered in the last few years as house prices have decreased beyond their borrowing, i.e. they are in negative equity. These people are struggling to pay their mortgages, and repossessions are at their highest for years. Many of these homeowners bought at, or near to the top of the market in the years from 2004 to 2008, when banks were literally throwing money at anyone with a pulse, offering loans of up to 125% (e.g. Northern Rock) of loan to value. No equity or negative equity now means that these unfortunate people are caught in the 'property trap' and they cannot move! They *can't afford to sell* at today's more realistic prices without incurring a loss, sometimes leaving them with no other alternative than to throw the keys of their home back to the bank, be repossessed, or maybe even bankruptcy. How would that make you feel?

Therefore I have discovered a solution for these vendors and can help them, and other people who just can't get onto the property ladder, by providing them with a home, with the finance already in place despite their credit record, creating a *true win/win* situation for them, and a win for me too.

It was in helping as many people as possible out of

seemingly impossible situations that I found made me push the boundaries – and I will speak more of this later in the book.

In the meantime, let's get cracking...

Section 2

Getting Educated about Property

What you need to know

I started to go on 'free' property seminars. I found the first one on the Internet, sent in my details, and then received a phone call to ask if I would attend the £297 value seminar on '*Making My Fortune in the Property Market*'. Well, it all sounded rather good, so I said *"yes"*. I was then called two more times prior to the event to ensure I was attending; this should have told me to 'be aware'.

At 7 pm at a local hotel in Northampton, myself and three other people listened to a 'full on' sales pitch that lasted 45 minutes. The other three parties made their excuses and left, but I was hooked! After all, it was only £6,000 for attending a training session that would show me the way to make money in property! After all *"property doubles in value every seven years"* (their quote not mine) and the facts speak for themselves! AND if I paid £2,000 there and then, I could pay the remainder at only £100 per month.

Blimey, not two hours had passed, and I was already in debt by £6,000. Well, the course was okay, in fact, it was great. It would have been fantastic if it was relevant, but it was out of date. They were banging on about BMV (below market value) properties that you get from motivated sellers, keen to sell their home to you for around a 30% discount. Yeah right! But I didn't know any better, I believed in what I heard and later on, set out to do just that I advertised as shown, in local papers, put out flyers, and waited for the rush of desperate sellers.

Well, I got nowhere fast. Still not to be daunted, I pressed on with my next course. This one was a weekend event, attended by around 200 people, who had all paid around

£600 each. Well, *this was the most hideous weekend I have ever had.* It was all American razzamatazz, singing and dancing. It made me look and feel like a real idiot, promised the earth, and given nothing except, here it comes, the up sell... ONLY £12,000 for the real deal! Well, I crept away from that one.

Next up, **the franchise.** As an *experienced* franchiser with a lot of experience in franchising (see www.time4youfranchise.com) I thought this must be good. Wrong! It was a disaster waiting to happen, and I was determined I wasn't going to get stung, even though the guy charged me £250 just to meet him, so that he didn't waste his time interviewing me if I wasn't suitable! That was too expensive; £250 for one hour's waste of my own time plus the expense of an overnight in a hotel up north.

Ultimately, I got around to attending some good events that taught me more. The feeling I got from the free events was that the sales pitch was never far away, and while anyone could garner enough information to piece it all together and then jump in and actually do something, most of the attendees didn't ever start. I subsequently found out that around 95% of attendees at free (or paid for) seminars never ever started – a real shame.

After attending event after event, I quickly concluded that even if I did get smart and start, I knew that the least educated person with a steely resolve could get somewhere if they could find these elusive motivated sellers, whereas if I became *the* most educated of property investors, yet never spoke to anyone because of a lack of leads, then I'd also be doomed to fail. The answer as I saw it was in marketing.

3 Important questions you need to ask yourself.

- Are you ready?
- Are you willing?
- Are you able?

Ready, willing and able, easy to say - but ask yourself, <u>ARE YOU?</u>

Ready to commit time, effort and perseverance?

<u>Willing</u> to step outside your comfort zone and do stuff that you may find uncomfortable, that you may not even really believe works, but do it anyway?

<u>Able</u> to find the time required, and if need be, to fund this learning experience?

Be absolutely honest here, because without a genuine desire and resolve, you too may just become a course junkie and <u>reverse</u> your fortunes.

The next book I read was '*Investing in Real Estate With Lease Options and "Subject-To" Deals*', an all-American book by *Wendy Patton*. This was a road map, pure and simple. Take out the obvious references to the market in the USA and everything was laid out for me. With lease options you are able to control properties without buying them, so obviously the potential to profit is brilliant, and the costs of getting started are really low.

I would recommend this book as the second book you read after '*Rich Dad, Poor Dad.*'

Having read both you just need to get <u>doing</u> something to help you get where you want to be.

What I Achieved

The sum total of my year was as follows: I had a personal target of 12 properties within 12 months, and I achieved nine. So I failed, or did I? I did acquire nine properties, that meant an annual increase of £24,400 plus four one-off payments equalling £11,000. All in all £35,400 of which £24,400 being passive income for the next ten years, resulting in £244,000! Not bad eh?!

How would that make <u>you</u> feel?

What I didn't mention were all the calls that <u>didn't</u> result in sales. Why didn't I mention them? Because they didn't matter to me - the only ones that mattered to me were the ones that I actually got, bearing in mind that as I'm actually still alive, I can do it again next year and if I choose, following years too!

However, my personal goal was, and still is, £50,000 over and above what I currently earn, and to get that money for as many years as I can, that for me is my personal freedom.

Now, let's take a look into your personal freedom, wants and needs.

What Do You Want?

How much is enough?

Most people believe that more money is needed <u>before</u> they start to invest in themselves and their future, but how much is enough? £100? £1,000? £10,000? £100,000? Personally, I believe that you can start to learn about property investing with as little as £10. You've already started at that amount with this book!

But it's more about actually starting than waiting until you have your 'enough' money, as when you do have enough, you won't want to risk losing it by making the wrong decisions because of your perceived lack of experience.

Warren Buffett

Warren Buffett is a multi-billionaire, but I'm guessing he didn't start out as one. He just did it in bite-sized pieces, just like I've just done. I may have missed my target of 12 properties but I have ended up with nine, plus much more relevant experience to see me through to my eventual goal of an extra £50,000 per year.

One of his famous rules were as follows:

2 Critical Rules you must never forget

Rule No 1 Never lose money

Rule No 2 Never forget rule No 1

The one thing I didn't suffer from was procrastination, nor do I over analyse things. For a start, I always make a to-do list every day! This one simple thing helps me focus on what I need to do, and get things done. If for any reason something hasn't been struck off my list, as done that day, it will be the No 1 thing to get done the next day.

> My top tip to you is to do this one really simple
> thing to help you get more focused, and achieve
> more, bit by bit.

How to get moving forward

The next time you have a problem you could think like a kid for ten minutes, and get the problem sorted. Or if you are the type of person who over-analyses everything, you could spend the next two hours doing a full cost-analysis, flow-chart the progress, a time-frame projection, and consider the human resources departmental breakdown flip-chart summary!!

In other words, *make a list of things to do, and then ensure you do them.*

My year for me was started with a list

➲ I started working on my list.

➲ I did a bit each day I had available.

➲ I completed my first full year.

➲ I got somewhere.

IF you want to create a fantastic future, then you'd better start working on it ***Right Now!***

The nuts and bolts follow on from here. Please stay with me and let me help you with your shiny new future.

Section 3

Personal Case Studies

In this section I am going to be sharing with you the properties I acquired, including all the headaches that came with them. I have included them in my book so that you can see exactly what I did, what worked and what didn't and hopefully you'll learn some important lessons along the way.

Property Nos 1 and 2

Property No 1 was very important to me, as I wanted to start immediately! No waiting around for me. So, I contacted a property finder service that advertised on-line (these guys find suitable properties and refurbish them). All I needed to do was to have £30,000 available. This would then cover the deposit, the refurbishment and the property finder's fees. Sounded simple enough.

The sales pitch is something along these lines: *"We buy at below market value, we arrange everything for you including the refurbishments, you provide the initial funds, you then let it out via our letting agency. After six months you then apply for a re-mortgage (as the house should have increased in value). You then get your initial investment back, you re-invest in another property and so on and after a few short years, you would have a property portfolio worth £1 million plus and an income from rents at around £30,000 per year!"* All this, while sitting watching the telly!

So, there I was, keen as mustard to get going. I acquired my first property, a nice looking three bedroom semi-detached Victorian property. Within two weeks I wanted another, which meant another £30,000.

Property No 2 was a two-bedroom terrace built around

1975, and after a couple of months, both were ready.

The first one was let immediately, but the second wasn't let for over *six months*! I was also paying two mortgages; receiving one rent (less letting agent fees, plus VAT) plus the Council tax on property number 2 because it was empty. Finally, I had a call from the letting agency, stating that they had an enquiry from a company that worked with the Government and needed my 2nd property to let on a 'corporate let,' for a term of five years. *Brilliant!* That soon ended my worry over that particular property.

What actually transpired was an <u>absolute nightmare!</u>

The agent was absolutely clueless; she signed the Assured Short-Hold Tenancy on my behalf and then told me that the corporate letting company wanted a furniture package, not to exceed £1,200. So, reluctantly I said yes, after all, I was going to get five years of rent, so what the hell?

In the event, I got hit with a massive bill for nearly £3,000. Refrigerator, <u>double</u> the price for furniture, curtains, *burglar alarm*, complete with a yearly maintainence contract. Special film to be applied to the front elevation windows so people could not see inside, plus £600 for cleaning! Well, I went loopy, I demanded to know what was happening, and was told that the house was being prepared for an asylum seeker. Now I have nothing against asylum seekers but, as far as I know, asylum seekers are not allowed to work, so why then can't they do the cleaning themselves? They have got nothing else to do all day long have they? As they are not allowed to work, and who would want to burgle them, all they have is the stuff paid for by me. Not only that, but the silly letting agent signed on my behalf that they (the company renting) would pay two months in arrears! Then, as if it really could not get any worse, I found I could not re-mortgage the house, as the building society would not accept the <u>AST Rental Agreement</u>, as it was not standard! So, I fired the letting agent, and gave the corporate company and their asylum seeker the required two months' notice to quit. Back to square one!

I now have a 'normal' letting agent with a 'normal' tenant but when it came to re-mortgage, neither properties qualified for what I was led to believe (my initial investment) which meant I was seriously over budget. The total I got back was £25,000 out of £60,000 initially invested. Ouch! I learned a lesson with those two properties.

What have you learned from my mistakes here?

 Not sure what the lessons are? Go to www.freddierayner.com/casestudies for *'Freddie's Lessons Learnt'* PDF - download it today!

Property No 3

Property No 3 was acquired during the time that I was trying to sort my 'property done for me' business, by using the property finders service; A guy called me, having got my number from one of the 'I buy houses' flyers I had been delivering. This property was closer to home, a reasonable three bedroom house, in a not too bad an area. He told me that he was in a **negative-equity** situation, meaning that he owed more on the mortgage than the house was worth, plus he was £3,500 in arrears! I considered it over a weekend then got back to him and offered to 'take it off his hands'.

He was delighted!

To make it legal I paid him £1 for it.

I then settled the arrears of £3,500 and paid his and my own Solicitor's fees. Unfortunately for me, I then found out that the real reason he had sold it was that he had a tenant, one that hadn't paid the rent for over a year, and now he was my tenant. So, I went around to see him – he was massive! I'm six-foot tall, and this guy was about six inches taller and two feet wider, and I was beginning to wish that I hadn't gone on my own – and at night. Anyway, I told him that I was the new owner of the property and I wanted him out. I said I would forget about the rent he owed, and would <u>GIVE</u> him £250 to leave within one month. I then said that if he didn't go, I'd pay someone the £250 to <u>make</u> him leave. He looked at me and said *"I can't go 'cos I haven't got a landlord's reference and I need it to rent another place"*. So, I said I would get him one typed out, and I delivered it by hand the next day.

Well, the month went by and he still hadn't moved, so I issued a <u>Section 21 Notice</u>, which is the term for possession proceedings (more money to the Solicitors). That took two months! If he was to still there after two months, we then had to apply to the Court for possession (another month at least) plus more Solicitors' costs. Thankfully he left, he didn't tell me of course. I went round to the house to see if he had gone, knocked on the door, no answer. I asked the neighbours if they knew anything, but of course they didn't. I then started to bash down the front door, and three minutes later along came the police, wanting to know why my 14lb lump hammer was being used instead of a key. After a phone call to my Solicitor they left me to it.

Now the house was *finally mine*, trashed of course, but I didn't mind, as I expected as much. I got my team onto it immediately, and set about making it presentable and ready to sell on as a **Rent-to-Buy**.

I found a tenant buyer in less than four weeks, £2,500 cash up-front, £200 monthly *cash flow for 120 months (10 years), then £3,000 **back-end profits. This was a **'Rent-to-Own'** option deal.

> A lesson learned from this one – find out what is really going on <u>before</u> you spend any money.

Property No 4

Property No 4 came my way as a result of me putting up a sign on my van that I'd parked in my local Tesco. A young lady had bought her house a few years ago on a 100% mortgage at £107,000, which was now worth £95,000.

She wanted to move quickly as she and her boyfriend wanted to live together and he lived in Bicester, some 40 miles away. I said I would take over the debt, **paid her £1** and she vacated the property after one week.

She was delighted, and so was I.

This time, no tenants!

Within one month, I found a **tenant buyer** who couldn't get a mortgage. So my *'rent today and own later'* plan really helped her move from paying her landlord's mortgage, to a deal where she paid me market rent, plus a ***getting started' amount of £2,500.

For my part I had taken on someone else's mortgage of £430 per month (the option was £1), the new tenant buyer was paying market rent of £570, which then gave me a *cash flow of £140pm.*

The price she will pay in seven years' time is £110,000. She gave me £2,500 plus £140 cash flow over seven years and I will get £3,000 at the end of the term. She was delighted, and so was I! (Who wouldn't be be delighted at getting £17,260 for just a pound initial investment!)

This too was a **Rent-to-Own** option deal.

> Lesson learned – do it this way from now on!

Property No 5

Property No 5 was acquired about one week after the last property. I got this lead from someone who saw the advertising *on my car* and asked, *"Do you buy houses?"* Duh!

This chap was having trouble keeping a reliable tenant in his property, and was struggling to keep his head above the water, in regards to the mortgage. Even though the house was worth £125,000, I ended up agreeing to buy his house for £115,000, with an **Option to Purchase** in 5 years time. In the interim, I rented it from him for £500 per month.

So my offer seemed to take away all the pressures from him. I could see from the property layout that if I added a partition, and rented out on a room by room basis, I could really improve the cash flow, and all this without getting a mortgage! In this property I added the partition wall and got £980 in rent, and as I had to make the council tax payment of £105 per month, this house was making me £375 per month seemingly all out of thin air.

This was a £1 down 'Lease Option' strategy.

I would definitely do this one again!

So, what can you learn from this?

Property No 6

This man had seen my *leaflet* and phoned me on the telephone number printed on it, as he had had a company in, claiming to buy houses quickly, who had offered him £67,000 (the property was actually worth around £95,000, if it was tidied up and a given a bit of TLC), and he was looking for a better offer. I then asked him what his mortgage on the place was, he told me £27,000 but he had a second mortgage on it for £40,000. I asked him what he had spent it on, and he said he'd bought a caravan and a bigger, newer car with it – seven years ago! The car was a wreck and the caravan had long since disappeared. *What a waste!*

He gave me the details of his mortgage, the second charge details, and also signed a form giving me the authority to speak to the lenders on his behalf. I spoke to the second charge lender asking for a reduction in the amount owed, as he had to go to live with his daughter and needed some money from the sale of his house to take with him. Basically, the second lender told me to go away, as they would not reduce the outstanding amount. I asked them to please put it in writing to either me, or their client, to which they asked why. I said that I need that letter in case their client ever ended up in Court, and the Judge could see what greedy bastards they were – they hung up on me. Two days later the guy phoned me up and said, "Wow, thanks for that". I asked *"For what?"* He then told me that second charge lender had reduced the outstanding balance owed by £6,000, and he was delighted. I then told him that I would pay him £4,000 more than his last quote, which would then mean he would have £10,000 in his pocket.

I bought that house for £71K with a '**Buy-to-Let**' mortgage of £53K

It makes £360 per month cash flow, and over 10 years, that will <u>mean £43K plus</u>.

I can then sell it for the market value, which could be around £120K, giving me an *additional £67K!* (£120,000 sale minus £53K mortgage)

<u>That is a £110K profit over 10 years – not bad eh?</u>

That was a '**BMV Deal**' (below-market-value), hard to

find, but great when you get them.

 So what did you learn from this one? Go to www.freddierayner.com/casestudies for *'Freddie's Lessons Learnt'* PDF - download it today!

Property No 7

I had a call from a guy who had seen my *'bandit board'*, (I explain what that is in Section 4) and we met up at my local Costa Coffee for a chat about how I could help him resolve his property headache.

He had split up from his wife; they had both moved out of the property they shared, and then rented it out, but the tenants failed to keep up with the rent payments, leaving him with the letters demanding payment of mortgage arrears. It got worse. The arrears mounted up and the tenants did a 'flit' and left the place in a right old mess, leaving him owing £120K plus £6K of arrears.

I agreed to take the debt of £120K off his hands, and he agreed to pay off the arrears. The house needed a good clean up, a lick of paint, grass cut and so on, nothing too challenging, costing around £500. The mortgage had 27 years to run at £550 per month, and the rental value was £650 per month. This was offered as a '**Rent-to-Buy**', £3,000 up-front, £200 per month cash flow and £9,000 *back-end* profit over 10 years.

This strategy is the one I liked best of all, everyone wins, and it really is a great feeling.

Property No 8

It was at this point that I started my website.

This meant that I could get potential leads from anywhere in the UK – and I did.

I had a call from a woman who wanted to move to Scotland – *very fast*. (She lived in Hull.)

The property was valued by **RICS (Royal Institute of Chartered Surveyors)** at £78K and the mortgage owed was £56K. As I was not really bothered about a house so far away, I decided to ask her if she would sell the property to me for what she owed on it, if I paid the Solicitors costs. I held my breath but she agreed!

I got a standard **Buy-to-Let** mortgage, and rented it out almost immediately for £220 per month cash flow. That will mean that over the 10-year period I have the Buy-to-Let mortgage, I will make £26,400, plus the difference on the eventual sale price and the outstanding mortgage, which should make me an extra £40K.

Not bad, and I never even saw the property! It was all handled by Solicitors and then a local letting agent, costing just 8% plus VAT – well worth it!

Property No 9

This was a lead from a leaflet drop last year.

A couple called me up and invited me round to have a chat about their situation. They had decided to split up and live elsewhere, getting on with their own lives without each other. All they wanted was £5K each from the house sale.

The property was on the market for £130K, and they had a mortgage of £120K, so in their eyes they had *£10,000 in equity*. All they needed to do was find an estate agent who would sell the house for *full market value*, (when everyone else was selling for less than market value to achieve a sale). What they could not see was that the place was a dump and it smelt of cats' wee. I could smell it, any potential client would smell it and so it remained unsold.

I asked them breezily, how the house sale was going? *"Not very well,"* they replied. *"Any viewings?"* I asked. *"Just a few,"* they said. *"Any offers?"* I asked. *"None,"* they said. *"Why do you think that could be?"* I asked. They both looked at each other, then at me and said, *"Because other people can afford to sell their properties for less, that's why."* Then I asked them, *"So when all the cheaper properties have been sold, yours will be the next to sell, don't you think?"* They thought about it and said, *"Well, we don't want to live together any more, we've met other partners and we want to get shot of this place really fast, and your leaflet said that's what you do!"*

I then asked them if they would prefer me to pay the next mortgage payment, or would they like to pay it? They both agreed that they would prefer me to pay their next mortgage payment. I then asked them how many years were left on it, the reply was 22 years. Who would they prefer to pay the remaining 22 years of mortgage payments, them or me?

Of course, they decided they would like me to pay the next 22 years of mortgage payments. At that point, I took out a *one pound coin*, put it on the table and said, *"If you accept this one pound coin as payment for your 22 years of debt, then you will have just sold your house, and can get on with the rest of your life, without the burden of this debt, how would that make you feel?"* They looked at each other, then at me, and said, *"Thank you."*

The deal was done.

They moved out within two weeks, my cleaners moved in, so did the skip, then the carpenters, the decorators, the carpet fitters, and so on until the house was ready to be sold on to a **tenant buyer**. It took six weeks to find someone who wanted a clean, fresh-smelling three bedroom semi with a garage, front and rear gardens. He paid me £3K getting started money, £750 per month rental (which included a £120 ****top-up per month) That mortgage was a re-payment mortgage which meant that each mortgage payment made it effectively reduced the amount outstanding, therefore in 10 years, the amount outstanding to be repaid was £88K - (I had sold the property at an agreed price of £135K.) So the difference was mine (don't forget I also had the getting started amount and top up amount) being repaid which was roughly £60K - all for £1.

Interestingly, as tenant buyers, they never even asked me how much the property was being sold for, that was later after they'd moved in.

These people were really pleased with their own home, purchased with a **rent now, pay later** option. The deal was worth £60K to me over 10 years; I could have gone 20 years and made much more money, but everyone got what they wanted.

Win! Win! Win!

That was another £1 **lease option** deal (see next section for an example of this).

*__Cash flow__ refers to what I was making over the base rate of what I was paying. So, for example, if I was charging £450 a month rent, but was only paying £250 mortgage, then I'm gaining £200 a month *cash flow*.

I refer to cash flow in all of my examples, so please bear that in mind.

**__Back-end__ profit is the money you earn at the end of the term (or end of the deal).

*** __Getting started or Front end__ amount refers to the money you get at the beginning of the deal.

****__Top-up amount__ is a something I offer my tenant buyers. Basically, they can pay the basic monthly amount due (rent) but if they wish, an additional amount that will go towards the deposit when they come to buy. This amount accumulated just gets deducted from the amount they owe on the property.

Section 4

An example of a Lease Option

Basically, a **lease option** is a lease (rent) with an *option to buy*. The term of the lease is negotiable, but usually determined by the length of mortgage left on the property. I have several over seven years, one over 27 years, and two over 10 years. The future purchase price is also agreed prior to signing, and then the property can be bought at *any time within the option term*. The option is exactly that, 'an option'. So, I have the option to buy, but not the obligation. The seller, on the other hand, does not have an option; *he has the obligation to sell*. Correctly worded, via a solicitor, all options are assignable, which means you can sell them on, for a fee of course.

Here is an example of one lease option I've actually done. *The first part* is what I've agreed with the seller. *The next is what the Solicitor came up with from my one-page agreement.*

Example

This is a simple one-page document that you could create freehand on a blank bit of A4 paper. As I have shown here, all that I have put down is what is agreed to, by both the sellers and myself. The purpose of this is to show that you are not being too clever, not trying to get them to sign papers with 'legal' stamped all over them, and it looks really simple to sign.

What follows on from that is what I then receive from my solicitor, and that is anything but simple, but it is the next logical hurdle to get over, as the sellers are now on your side, they want their pain to go away, and you represent the solution for them.

Heads of Terms

Home owners name: DAVID MICHAEL SMITH

Address of Property to be leased:
3, The Nice House
Wellingborough
North Hants
ND8 3FB

Current Address:
5 Smithfield Terrace
Wellingborough
North Hants
ND9 5PA

Agreement Fee: £1.00

Length of Term: 204 Months

Purchase Price: £94,934.99

Purchasors details: Frederick David Rayner
19 Standing Stones
Gt Billing
Northampton
NN3 9HA

Email: freddie.rayner@timeforyou.co.uk

Date: 14 Sept 2012

Signed by home owner   Signed by purchaser

_____   _____

DATED SEPT 12TH 2012

OPTION TO Purchase

relating to

3 THE NICE HOUSE WELLINGBOROUGH ND8 3FB

between

DAVID MICHAEL SMITH

and

FREDERICK DAVID RAYNER

THIS DEED is dated   2012

PARTIES

(1)   David Michael Smith of 5 Smithfield Terrace
       Irthlingborough ND9 5PA (Seller)

(2)   Frederick David Rayner of 19 Standing Stones
       Northampton NN3 9HA (Buyer)

BACKGROUND

The Seller owns the property known as 3 The Nice House,
Wellingborough ND8 3FB and has agreed to grant the
Buyer an option to buy it in accordance with the terms of
this Deed.

AGREED TERMS

1.   INTERPRETATION

1.1   The definitions in this clause apply in this Deed.

Buyer's Solicitors:

Completion Date: Means the date which is 20
working days after service of the Option Notice on
the Seller

Conditions: The Standard Conditions of Sale
(Fourth Edition) and Condition means any one of
them.

Initial Option Fee: £1

Insurance Policy: The buildings insurance policy
in respect of the Property underwritten by the
Insurer (a copy of which has been provided to the
Buyer prior to the date of this Deed) or such other

insurance policy as may be obtained by the Buyer in accordance with clause 6.

Insurer: Such company or organisation which provides the Insurance Policy.

Mortgage: The mortgage secured on the Property dated 18 August 2006 in favour of the Mortgagee.

Mortgage Payments: The monthly sums payable from time to time during the Option Period under the terms of the Mortgage to the Mortgagee.

Mortgagee: Mortgages 1 Limited (Co. Regn. No. 3186649) of Mortgages PLC Bank of America Merrill Lynch Financial Centre 2 King Edward Street London EC1A 1HQ.

Option: The option granted by the Seller to the Buyer by this Deed.

Option Notice: Written notice exercising the Option in the form or substantially in the form set out in Schedule 1 to this Deed.

Option Period: The period of 204 months from and including the date of this Deed.

Power of Attorney: Means the irrevocable Power of Attorney entered into pursuant to clause 5.7 a certified copy which is attached to this Deed.

Property: The freehold property known as 3 The Nice House Wellingborough ND8 3FB which is registered at HM Land Registry under title number NN226413.

Purchase Price: £94,934.99

Sellers Solicitor:

Tenancy: Means an assured shorthold tenancy of the Property granted on terms materially similar to those set out in Schedule 2.

Working Day: any day from Monday to Friday (inclusive) which is not Christmas Day, Good Friday, a statutory Bank Holiday or a Jewish holiday.

1.2   The rules of interpretation in this clause apply in this Deed.

1.3   Clause and Schedule headings do not affect the interpretation of this Deed.

1.4   Except where a contrary intention appears, a reference to a clause or a Schedule is a reference to a clause of, or Schedule to this Deed.

1.5   Unless otherwise specified, a reference to a law is a reference to it as it is in force for the time being taking account of any amendment, extension, application or re-enactment and includes any subordinate legislation for the time being in force made under it.

1.6   A person includes a corporate or unincorporated body.

1.7   Words importing one gender shall be construed as importing any other gender.

1.8   Words importing the singular shall be construed as importing the plural and vice versa.

1.9   Where any party comprises more than one person the obligations and liabilities of that party under this Deed shall be the joint and several obligations and liabilities of those persons.

1.10   Writing or written includes faxes but not e-mail.

1.11   Any obligation in this Deed on a person not to do something includes an obligation not to agree or allow that thing to be done.

1.12   Any reference to the Seller or to the Buyer includes their respective personal representatives and successors in title.

2.   OPTION

2.1   On the date of this Deed the Buyer will pay the Initial Option Fee to the Sellers (receipt of which is hereby acknowledged by the Seller).

2.2   In consideration of

    (a)   the Initial Option Fee paid by the Buyer to the Seller;

    (b)   the Mortgage Payments paid by the Buyer to the Mortgagee; and

    (c)   the obligations entered into by the Buyer under this Deed the Seller grants to the Buyer an option during the Option Period to buy the Property at the Purchase Price.

2.3   The Buyer may assign the benefit of this Option to a third party provided that he gives written notice of such assignment together with the assignee's name and address to the Seller within 5 working days of the assignment.

2.4   The Buyer may novate the benefits and obligations
       of this Option in favour of a third party provided
       that he gives written notice of such novation
       together with the third party's name and address to
       the Seller within 5 working days of the assignment.
       The Seller hereby appoints the Buyer as its attorney
       for the purpose of executing any deed of novation
       on such terms as the Buyer may agree in its absolute
       discretion and a third party shall be entitled without
       enquiry to assume that the events causing this
       power of attorney to be exercisable have arisen.

2.5   Any monies paid by the Buyer pursuant to this Deed
       are not refundable to the Buyer in any
       circumstances save for where the Seller has
       breached any or all of the terms of this Deed and
       not rectified such breach within 21 days of written
       notice from the Buyer and to the Buyer's reasonable
       satisfaction in which case any such monies are
       refundable to the Buyer upon demand.

2.6   The Seller will (at the Buyer's cost) promptly give
       all assistance required by the Buyer in relation to a
       sale of the Property, to include (but not limited to)
       completing and signing any paperwork, replying to
       pre-contract enquiries, replying to requisitions on
       title, obtaining mortgage redemption figures,
       providing statutory declarations (if required) and
       dealing promptly with any Land Registry
       requisitions.

2.7   For the avoidance of doubt the obligation of the
       Buyer to make the Mortgage Payments as herein

detailed shall not extend to redemption or repayment of the Mortgage or payment of any arrears existing prior to the date of this Deed.

3.   **DEPOSIT**

If an Option Notice is served the Buyer shall pay a deposit of £1.00 to the Seller's Solicitors or if they are no longer instructed the solicitors acting for the Seller and the Buyer undertakes to notify the Buyer in writing of the same.

4.   **BUYER'S OBLIGATIONS AND UNDERTAKINGS**

During the Option Period:

4.1   The Buyer will pay the Mortgage Payments to the Mortgagee in accordance with the terms of the Mortgage.

4.2   The Buyer will maintain the Property in no worse state of decoration and repair than the state at the date of this Deed excluding any structural repairs.

4.3   The Buyer will pay and indemnify the Seller against:

(a)   all rates taxes assessments duties charges impositions and outgoings which are now or during the Option Period are charged assessed or imposed on the Property or on the owner or occupier of it other than payable by the Sellers in connection with any dealing with or disposition of the title to the Property or any legal fees in relation to the sale of the Property;

(b)   all charges for electricity gas water and other services consumed or used at the Property (including meter rents) during the Option Period; and

(c)   all costs expenses and demands arising from a Tenancy including (but not limited to) the costs of complying with all statutes and laws in relation to the Tenancy and obtaining a court order for possession of the Property and enforcement of that order and all steps preliminary to obtaining possession including the service of any notices under any Housing Act.

4.4   The Buyer will not make any further drawings nor apply for any further borrowings under the terms of the Mortgage or use the Property as security for any other borrowing.

4.5   The Buyer will not permit or suffer anybody to reside at or occupy the Property unless such person or persons have first entered into a Tenancy.

4.6   The Buyer will not change the locks to the Property without the prior consent of the Seller (such consent not to unreasonably withheld or delayed) and, if such consent is given, the Buyer will change the locks at his own cost and supply a copy of keys for all new locks to the Seller within 5 Working Days of the change of locks.

4.7   The Buyer will not be required to pay any monies or incur any liability in relation to any matters which have occurred or commenced in any part prior to the date hereof.

4.8   The Buyer will not be required to pay any arrears or

costs existing under the terms of the Mortgage at the date hereof or which are applied to the Mortgage account by the Mortgagee at any time in respect of any arrears existing prior to the date hereof.

5. SELLER'S OBLIGATIONS AND UNDERTAKINGS

5.1 The Seller shall not create or dispose of any legal or equitable interest (including without limitation any easement right of covenant) in on over or under nor create any right or licence to occupy or use the Property or any part of it without the prior written consent of the Buyer, such consent not to be unreasonably withheld or delayed.

5.2 The Seller shall not sell or agree to sell the Property without the prior written consent of the Buyer.

5.3 The Seller shall not make any further drawings nor apply for any further borrowings under the terms of the Mortgage or any other finance to be secured on the Property.

5.4 From the date of this Deed the Seller hereby authorises all rents and any other sums due from any tenants of the Property from time to time be paid directly to the Buyer and to be retained by the Buyer solely as a profit to the Buyer as part consideration for the Buyer entering into this Deed and upon the date of this Deed will provide a letter to the current tenants (if any) of the Property authorising all future rent payments to be made to the Buyer

5.5   The Seller grants the Buyer authority to:

(a)   grant a Tenancy of the Property to any third
party at the Buyer's discretion pursuant to the
terms of the Power of Attorney; and

(b)   enter the Property at any time Provided That
the Buyer shall not reside at or occupy any part
of the Property (with or without others) unless
he has entered into a Tenancy.

5.6   The Seller shall not from the date of this Deed
without the prior written consent of the Buyer (such
consent not to be unreasonably withheld or
delayed) occupy or enter the Property.

5.7   On the date of this Deed the Seller will sign and
deliver to the Buyer the Power of Attorney.

6. MORTGAGE AND INSURANCE

6.1   The Buyer shall during the Option Period keep the
Property insured for its full reinstatement value
against loss or damage by the risks required by the
Council of Mortgage Lenders' Handbook.

6.2   The Buyer will insure the Property either in the
name of the Seller with the Buyer's proprietary
interest noted or in the joint names of the Seller and
the Buyer.

6.3   The Buyer will:

(a)   give the Insurance Company notice
immediately of any matter that occurs of
which he is aware that any insurer or
underwriter may treat as material in deciding
whether or on what terms to insure or to

continue to insure the Property;

(b)   not do or omit anything as a result of which any policy of insurance of the Property or any neighbouring property may become void or voidable or otherwise prejudiced, or the payment of any policy money may be withheld;

(c)   comply at all times with the requirements of the Insurance Company relating to the Property; and

(d)   give the Seller and Insurance Company immediate notice of the occurrence of any damage or loss of which he is aware relating to the Property of which he is aware arising from an insured risk or of any other event that might affect any insurance policy relating to the Property.

6.4   The Buyer shall, subject to obtaining all necessary planning and other consents, use all insurance money received (other than for loss of rent) to repair the damage for which the money has been received or (as the case may be) in rebuilding the Property. The Buyer shall not be obliged to:

(a)   provide accommodation identical in layout or design so long as accommodation reasonably equivalent to that previously at the Property is provided; or

(b)   repair or rebuild the Property after a notice has been served pursuant to clause 6.5.

6.5   If, following damage to or destruction of the

Property, the Buyer reasonably considers that it is impossible or impractical to reinstate the Property, the Buyer may terminate this option by giving notice to the Seller. On giving notice this option shall determine but this shall be without prejudice to any right or remedy of either party in respect of any prior breach of this Deed. After repayment of the Mortgage and any other charges registered against the Property the proceeds of the insurance (other than any insurance for plate glass) shall be divided between the parties in accordance with the value of their respective interests in the Property, and if the parties cannot agree, the matter will be referred to an independent arbitrator agreed between the parties and if not so agreed, to be appointed by the president of the Royal Institution of Chartered Surveyors (RICS) and the decision of the arbitrator shall be final and binding on the parties (save in the case of manifest error) and his costs shall be borne as he shall direct.

6.6 On the initial implementation, amendment to or any renewal of the Insurance Policy the Buyer must send a copy of the amended or renewed policy to the Seller within 5 Working Days of such amendment or renewal.

7. EXERCISE OF THE OPTION

7.1 The Buyer may exercise the Option at any time during the Option Period by serving an Option Notice on the Seller or the Seller's Solicitors.

7.2 If the Option is exercised in accordance with the terms of this Deed the Seller will sell and the Buyer will buy the Property for the Purchase Price on the terms of this Deed.

7.3 The Seller by way of security irrevocably appoints the Buyer as his attorney for the duration of the Option Period for the purposes of giving effect to the completion of the sale and purchase of the Property pursuant to this Deed including (without limitation) signing the Transfer Deed to transfer the Property to the Buyer or a third party purchaser of the Buyer's nomination.

8. REGISTRATION

8.1 The Seller consents to the registration of an agreed notice or a unilateral notice in the Charges Register of the Seller's title to the Property.

8.2 The Seller consents to the Buyer making an application to the Land Registry on Form RX1 (or equivalent from time to time) to register a Restriction in the following form:

"No disposition of the registered estate by the proprietor of the registered estate is to be registered without a certificate signed by Frederick David Rayner or his conveyancer that the terms of an Option date   2012 and made between David Michael Smith (1) and Frederick David Rayner (2) have been complied with"

8.3 If the Option expires or is lawfully determined the Buyer shall within 21 days cancel registration of all notices and restrictions registered in the Registers of the Seller's title. Should the Buyer fail to comply with his obligation under this clause the Buyer appoints the Seller as its attorney for the purpose of applying to cancel the registered notice(s) and restriction(s) and a third party shall be entitled without enquiry to assume that the events causing this power of attorney to be exercisable have arisen.

9. TERMINATION

9.1 If during the Option Period the Buyer shall fail to pay any monies properly due pursuant to this Deed on the due date and has not rectified such failure within 21 days of the due date, the Seller shall be entitled to immediately terminate this Deed on the understand that there will be no obligation on the Seller to reimburse any monies paid by the Buyer pursuant to this Deed.

9.2 The Seller shall be entitled to rescind this Deed if the Buyer:

(a) (if a body corporate or, if more than one body corporate, any one of them) has a receiver or an administrative receiver appointed in respect of all or any part of its assets, or has an order made or a resolution passed for a winding-up (other than for the purpose of amalgamation or reconstruction not involving a diminution of assets), or notice of appointment of an administrator is filed at court in respect of it; or

(b) (if an individual or, if more than one individual, any one of them) becomes bankrupt, or has an interim order under Part VIII of the Insolvency Act 1986 made against him or has an interim receiver of his property appointed under section 286 of that 1986 Act; then in any such case the Seller is entitled to r escind this Deed by giving three Working Days' notice to the Buyer and at the expiration of such notice this Deed ends and the parties are released from any further liability under it but without cancelling any liability for an antecedent breach of this Deed.

9.3 On determination of this Deed (howsoever determined) the Buyer must immediately return all keys to the Property to the Seller.

9.4 The Buyer may also be entitled to immediately rescind this Deed if or where the Seller is an individual, individuals or a partnership and an order is made for the bankruptcy of the Seller (or any one of the person who constitute the Seller).

9.5 The termination of this Deed shall not affect any rights of the Seller or the Buyer which accrued up to the date of termination.

10. TITLE GUARANTEE

The Seller will transfer the Property with full title guarantee.

11. CONDITIONS

11.1 Upon exercise of the Option, the Conditions will be incorporated in this Deed in so far as they:

(a) apply to a sale by private treaty;

(b) relate to freehold property;

(c) are not inconsistent with the other clauses in

this Deed; and

(d)   have not been modified by the other clauses in this Deed.

11.2   The Conditions are supplemented and amended as follows:-

1.3.7   The following words shall be added: "(f) by hand: on delivery"

3   The Seller's duty of disclosure shall relate only to incumbrances of which the Seller has actual knowledge and in any event the word "and could not reasonably" in Condition

3.1.2   (c)   shall be deleted.

3.1.2   (d)   Shall be extended to include:

(i)   all local land charges (whether or not registered before the date of this Deed) and all matters capable of registration as local land charges;

(ii)   all notices, contracts, charges, conditions, demands, orders or requirements relating to planning legislation or other requirements of any public authority whether or not before the date of this Deed;

(iii)   all matters revealed or which might reasonably be expected to be revealed by the searches and enquiries which a prudent buyer ought to make, whether or not actually made by the Buyer.

3.1.2   The following words shall be added: "(f)

overriding interests as defined in Schedule 3 of the Land Registration Act 2002."

4.3.2   Shall be omitted.

5.1.1   Shall not apply and the following condition shall be substituted:-

> If the Property is destroyed or damaged prior to actual completion and the proceeds of any insurance policy effected by or on behalf of the Buyer are reduced by reason of the existence of any policy effected by the Seller, the purchase price for the Property shall be abated by the amount of such reduction but this Condition shall not apply if the proceeds of the Seller's policy are applied towards the re-instatement of the Property pursuant to any statutory or contractual obligation.

5.1.2   Shall be omitted.

10.4   Money payable by the Buyer for chattels shall be paid to the Seller's solicitors on completion and shall be treated as money due on completion for the purposes of Conditions 6 and 7.

12.   BUYER'S ACKNOWLEDGEMENT OF CONDITION

The Buyer acknowledges that before the date of this contract, the Seller has given the Buyer and others authorised by the Buyer, permission and the opportunity to inspect, survey and carry out investigations as to the condition of the Property. The Buyer has formed its own view as to the

condition of   the Property,
accepts the condition of the Property   at
the date of this Deed and the suitability of the
Property for the Buyer's purposes.

13. VACANT POSSESSION

13.1 The Property will be sold with vacant possession on completion unless a Tenancy subsists at the date of Completion in which case the Property will be sold subject to such Tenancy.

13.2 The Seller will provide vacant possession of the Property to the Buyer from the date hereof.

14. TRANSFER

14.1 The Transfer shall include the following provisions:

14.2 "This Transfer is made with full title guarantee but the covenants set out in section 3(1) of the Law of Property (Miscellaneous Provisions) Act 1994 shall not extend to any charge, incumbrance or right about which the Transferor does not know";

14.3 The covenant set out in section 2(1)(b) of the Law of Property (Miscellaneous Provisions) Act 1994 shall extend to include the words "at the cost of the Transferee" in substitution for the words "at his own cost"; and

14.4 "For the purpose of section 6(2)(a) of the Law of Property (Miscellaneous Provisions) Act 1994 all matters now recorded in registers open to public inspection are to be considered within the actual knowledge of the Transferee".

14.5 The Buyer will be entitled to direct the Seller to

transfer the Property to a third party of the Buyer's choice on the terms of this Deed save for the price which be higher (but not lower) than the Purchase Price. The difference between the price in the Transfer to a third party and the Purchase Price (if any) will belong to the Buyer and will be paid to the Buyer on the date of such transfer.

15. COMPLETION

15.1 Completion will take place on the Completion Date.

15.2 On completion the Buyer will pay the Purchase Price to the Seller.

16. ENTIRE AGREEMENT

16.1 This Deed constitutes the entire Agreement and understanding of the parties and supersedes any previous Agreement or understanding between them relating to the subject matter of this Deed.

16.2 The Seller acknowledges and agrees that in entering into this Deed, the Buyer is relying upon the written replies given by the Seller's solicitors to any enquiries raised by the Buyer or its solicitors.

17. NOTICES

17.1 Any notice (including the Option Notice) given under this Deed must be in writing and signed by or on behalf of the party giving it and be served by delivering it personally or sending it by pre-paid first class post or recorded delivery or fax to the address and for the attention of the relevant party as follows:

(a) to the Seller at:

5 Archfield Terrace Irthlingborough NN9 5QA

or to the Seller's Solicitors or to such other address or fax number, or for the attention of such other person, as was last notified in writing by the Seller to the Buyer.

(b)　to the Buyer at:

19 Standing Stones Northampton NN3 9HA

or to such other address or fax number, or for the attention of such other person, as was last notified in writing by the Buyer to the Seller.

17.2　Any such notice shall be deemed to have been received:

(a)　if delivered personally, at the time of delivery.

(b)　in the case of pre-paid first class post or recorded delivery, on the second Working Day after posting; and

(c)　in the case of fax, at the time of transmission if sent before 4.30pm or on the next Working Day if sent after that time.

17.3　In proving service it shall be sufficient to prove that delivery was made or that the envelope containing the notice was properly addressed and posted as a prepaid first class or recorded delivery letter or that the fax message was properly addressed and transmitted, as the case may be.

17.4　A notice given under this Deed will not be validly s

served if sent by e-mail.

18. RIGHTS OF THIRD PARTIES

A person who is not a party to this Deed may not enforce any of its terms under the Contracts (Rights) of Third Parties Act 1999.

19. JURISDICTION AND GOVERNING LAW

This Deed shall be governed by and constructed in accordance with English Law and the parties submit to the jurisdiction of the English Courts.

20. CONFIDENTIALITY

This Deed and the terms thereof shall be confidential to the parties both before and after completion and except:-

20.1 with authority of the other;

20.2 so far as may be necessary for the proper performance of their obligations hereunder; or

20.3 as required by law or any relevant stock exchange ordered to do so by a court of competent jurisdiction HM Land Registry or HM Revenue and Customs neither party shall make or authorise the making of any announcement or publication concerning this Deed or any of its terms (either whole or in part) nor any comment or statement relating thereto without the prior written consent of the other as to the form and content of any such announcement publication comment or statement.

21. GENERAL

21.1 The parties hereto are not in partnership with each

other.

21.2   This Deed is for the benefit of the parties to it and is not intended to benefit or be enforceable by anyone else save where any assignment is permitted under the terms of this Deed.

This Deed has been entered into on the date stated at the beginning of it.

Schedule 1 The Option Notice

To:Seller

Dear Sirs

Pursuant to an Option ('the Deed') dated Sept 12th 2012 made between David Michael Smith (1) and Frederick David Rayner (2) relating to

Frederick David Rayner gives notice of the exercise of the Option contained in the Deed to buy the Property on the terms set out in the Deed.

Yours faithfully

Frederick David Rayner

IN WITNESS whereof this Deed has been duly executed by the parties hereto as a deed the day and year first before written

SIGNED as a DEED by <u>David Michael Smith</u> in the present of:

Witness Signature ....

Witness Name ....

Witness Address ....

Witness Occupation ....

SIGNED as a DEED by <u>Frederick David Rayner</u>   in the present of:

Witness Signature ....

<u>Wow!</u> Now that really is a lot to get through at a first meeting!

However, it is really, really simple to simply make an appointment and just get the sellers *autograph*, don't ask for a signature as it sounds too legal!

You can say something like *"Hi John, I've got the paperwork back from my solicitors, all I need now is your autograph, thanks, it won't take long now...see you later!"*

Keep it short, and simple (K.I.S.S)

Option Agreements

Whilst these instruments are extremely versatile and as flexible as you need, you should ensure that any options you draw up are with your solicitors and include the following.

(1) The names of all parties to the agreement (even if as in a divorcing couple, each must be named and must sign).

(2) Full property descriptions to include a title plan downloadable from Land Registry website.

(3) Option to purchase. The Agreement must state that this is an Option Agreement.

(4) Option fee. This must be stated even if it is only £1.00 for it to be legally binding.

(5) Option Period

The period agreed by you and the sellers.

(6) Extension of option

This is useful should your tenant buyer not exercise their option, thereby enabling you to remain in control of the property for longer than expected.

(7) Purchase price

Quite obvious really.

(8) Notice period to exercise option.

Usually two months' notice required to exercise option.

(9) Assignment of Option.

This really is a must have as this will allow you to assign (sell on) this deal to another investor if you wanted to trade it on for an immediate profit.

(10) Right of entry

To be included for right of entry for surveyors, tenant buyers, potential investors etc.

Section 5

Marketing Your Business

The whole point of marketing your newly established property business is to make the phone ring!

Get this bit right and you're *over 50% there!*

As I've previously mentioned, I run a domestic cleaning franchise (www.timeforyou.co.uk). Whilst I have had considerable success in helping many new franchises build up a successful domestic cleaning business from scratch (and earn an average of £65,000 per year in profits part-time!). None of my franchisees do any cleaning themselves.

During the training period, they discover that it is all about the marketing of their business, not the nuts and bolts of cleaning. All the marketing is done purely to make the phone ring and once we achieve that, the rest is relatively simple.

This is where my previous experience was very useful to my new business. *All I needed to do was to find a quick way to make the phone ring.*

I knew instinctively that if the phone rang often enough, and I could talk to people who were reacting to my marketing, it wouldn't be too long before we would both find 'common ground,' and simply talk to each other to work out what was required to make a sale. I didn't bother about the legal bit, that's what solicitors are for. When I went to talk to sellers about their property challenges I <u>listened,</u> and acted as a sounding board. They told me everything I needed to know, that *enabled me* to make all the right noises, to let them know that I could help them get on with their lives, and leave the property pain behind them. All I had with me was a plain A4 sheet of paper and a pencil (not a pen). I wrote on the top of the sheet *"Heads of Terms,"* and I then wrote what we agreed to do. They would sell to me for the balance of their debt, and I would pay the mortgage for the rest of the term, **plus pay them £1.00 (this was to make it legal.)** They then signed it, and then I would sign it. One copy, which I would then send it off to my solicitor, who would then do all the legal stuff and make it fit for purpose. The lease option was drafted up, and signed a couple of weeks later.

So, now I needed to get the phone to ring more often.

The people I was looking for would ideally already have their house up for sale with an estate agent. They would probably have had their house on the market for a few months or more, probably with hardly any viewings and no sensible (if any) offers.

Even more ideal for me would be that the estate agent wouldn't even know that the property was in negative equity, and the sellers owed more than the house was worth, so couldn't take an offer lower than the asking price, as this would mean that they would have to pay thousands of pounds to their mortgage company to be able to sell and move on with their lives. The other kind of ideal people would be those looking to relocate to another part of the country, or even emigrating to another country, and the last thing that these people wanted was to leave their property in the hands of tenants, who might not pay the rent, or not look after their property. What these people were looking for would be a buyer that would make a quick decision to buy their property fast, even for a discount.

Another group of people my marketing was aimed at were couples who had split up or were divorcing. The last thing that they wanted was to carry on living together, but because the house was in joint names they just couldn't afford to live apart! They also needed a quick and simple solution that enabled them to get on with their lives.

So, how do we reach these prospective clients?

4 Quick ways to market your business

1. Leafleting
2. Cards in corner shops
3. Bandit boards
4. Stickers

Leaflets

Firstly, leaflets have to go somewhere, not just anywhere!

Before you do anything, get a map of the area you want to work. A big map. See www.geoplan.com. These maps are expensive, but will last you for years.

Leafleting

The main marketing route for getting clients is leafleting, especially when starting in a new area. My years of experience has proved that this is the tried and tested way to gain prospects and to get your message across, to as many people as possible within your chosen area.

When your leaflet is dropped through a prospect's doors, it will either fulfil an immediate need, and therefore get an immediate response, or the prospective client will hold onto it and call you as their need becomes more and more pressing.

Leafleting also acts as information distribution; the more people read the leaflet, the more that your prospective clients have the opportunity to respond to it.

For every leaflet dropped, someone will read it. This is the very heart of your business, i.e. it's a numbers game. The more information distributed about your service by way of leaflet, the more things will begin to happen.

How much to leaflet

From my own experience with franchises across the UK, I would suggest that you would expect one enquiry per 1,000 leaflets. Obviously this would depend on your choice of leaflet, the area you are leafleting, and the prospective client's needs at the time of delivery. It is really, really important to know that you need to leaflet your area often, not seldom – once is never enough! Once every four months will pay off, trust me on this one.

How to distribute the leaflets

"A journey of a million miles begins with a single step." ~ Confucius.

Ideally you will deliver your leaflets personally, as there are many benefits to this.

- ✓ It's cheaper than paying someone else to do it.
- ✓ You get to know your area – door-by-door, street-by-street.
- ✓ You KNOW that your leaflets are being delivered, and to the right properties.
- ✓ Free exercise!

Also by doing this yourself, you will know by experience what is involved, and the rate at which leaflets can be delivered. This will be important for you particularly when you are paying other people to deliver them for you.

Do it yourself with a bit of help

This is the next logical step, exactly as above but with 'helpers' such as friends or family, but it will be probably be better to have paid helpers in the long run.

Using local newspapers

Local papers will often distribute leaflets for a fee per 1,000 leaflets, depending on area. A rough guide would be around £15 - £25 per 1,000 leaflets.

From bitter experience here, this would appear to be an attractive proposition, especially if you have a full-time job, or it's winter and raining. However, this is the least satisfactory method, as most leaflets are ignored, or not even delivered. It would make more sense to pay a trusted person more money, and know the job has been done.

Royal Mail Distribution

This method of distributing your information is an excellent way to get your leaflets delivered. The only issue here is the cost, at around £65 per 1,000 with a minimum of 100,000 (at the time of writing) it could prove costly, and would not be the way I would go about it.

Professional Distribution Companies

There may be some good companies out there. Be aware the ones that offer a low price, and an invoice up front! They are the ones that spend your money and ditch your leaflets!

If you intend to use professional companies only use the ones that have been personally recommended to you.

Examples of adverts for leaflet distributors.

Earn *Extra* Money

Delivering leaflets locally

Good rate paid

Suit active individuals

Please phone

(Your No here) ask for Bill

Example No 2

Leaflet Deliverers Required

Earn Extra Money

Delivering leaflets, Part-time

Hours to suit you

£35.00 per thousand

Plus bonus

Tel (your No here) ask for Mary

Block Method for distribution

In order to monitor your leaflet distribution and be able to see what area out-performs another and to ensure 100% coverage I suggest you adopt this method.

Step 1

Take your chosen territory and as much as possible try to divide it equally into four sections marked 1-4 (See diagram)

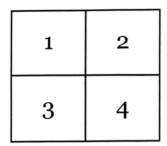

Step 2

In each of the four sections, sub divide into another four and label each as A, B, C and D (See diagram below).

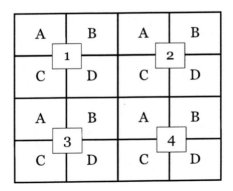

Step 3

Superimpose the territory over the block system as above; you will then have a defined area for distribution which may be identified by the block they are in.

This way you can now monitor particular areas where leaflets will be distributed.

For example you could distribute as follows:

1st Distribution   1A

2nd Distribution   4B

3rd Distribution   3C

4th Distribution   2D

5th Distribution   1D

6th Distribution   4D

7th Distribution   3B

Step 4

Create a monitor and response system where you record each distribution, how many leaflets used, how many responses received, and how often distribution is done. Doing it this way will help you really penetrate an area. Once you've done this once do it again, and again, and again. This pays dividends, and will help you achieve your goals, but only if you actually do it!

Franchisees have said "leaflets don't work, I've tried it once and got nothing from it!" But I have PROVEN that leaflets actually work! Unfortunately, you can't train the recipient to action the leaflets when you deliver them; it's all down to persistence and timing.

Whatever you do, do not be tempted to design your own, instead use leaflets that work! I've tried them out for you.

The leaflets I use have been designed with AIDA in mind. Aida isn't my old Auntie, it's an important acronym for:

- ➢ Attention
- ➢ Interest
- ➢ Desire
- ➢ Action

We have used this for the last fifteen years with 'Time for You' and we know what works from hard experience.

What you DON'T want to do is go down the usual Name, Rank, Serial number route. This leaflet talks all about the company, and not about the customer.

To see these leaflets in full colour, visit the website www.freddierayner.com/leaflets. These examples are designed very specifically, with the customer in mind, with clearly defined benefits.

Instead, you want your advertising to speak to the potential client.... and make the benefits clear.

Here is an example of one our housing leaflets that has worked well for us - notice the list of benefits beside the check marks.

This one has also done well.

Sell Your House TODAY!

Benefits Go Here

→ FREE Provisional Offer in 24hrs!
→ No Chain, Complete in 30 days!
→ Save in Legal Fees
→ Quick and Guaranteed Sale
→ No Equity? No Problem!
→ Avoid Repossession!

That's right, **TODAY!**

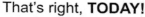

FREE Valuation & Consultation...............If You Call Before 30/06/12

Here to help you move on

Call or Text Sue for FREE Advice NOW
01234 567 890
Email: sue@emailaddress.co.uk
Website: www.YourWebSite.co.uk

So when you come to design your leaflets, please give some thought to AIDA and make sure that the benefits to your company are clear and easy to spot.

If you're still unsure of how to go about this, then look up AIDA marketing on the internet. There is lots of information about it, and it really will make a difference to your advertising.

Also, take a look at the suggested reading section at the back of this book.

Card in Corner shop

This is an example of a postcard that we put in local shops.

NEED TO SELL YOUR HOUSE FAST?

WE BUY HOUSES LOCALLY & PAY £7,000 MORE

PLEASE CALL SUE ON 01604 651008

Bandit Boards

I guess these are known as bandit boards because no one ever asks for permission to put them up!

These are correx flute yellow bards, with a hand written message as seen above. The point of these is to be seen to be different, not nice, not corporate, but different. I got my best deal from one of these boards, they get taken down by annoyed individuals or councils, but as you're not in this business for any awards for style, my advice is to stop worrying, just do it!

Stickers

These stickers are to be used within your area anywhere to reinforce your message.

Stick them on a postcard and place in your local newsagents, use them at bus stops, on ATM's, on estate agents boards, on wheelie bins, lampposts, near fish and chip shops, betting shops and around schools. Get them out there! Once you have paid to have them printed, they won't bring in single phone call unless you stick them up somewhere!

Telephone Service

If like me, you plan to start off in a part-time capacity, you will need to organise how your phone will be answered, when, and by whom.

All of your marketing is to make your phone ring, and if you are away from your phone because you are at work, or on another call, or (hopefully) with a prospective client and your prospective client hears a busy tone, they might never call back!

This will be your new business venture, so start out like a real business and get yourself sorted with a telephone answering service. Personally I would recommend Star Virtual tel (01933 462130). The owner, Frank, will help you by asking you to write down what you need his staff to say when answering your calls. They will then email and text you immediately they have received a call for you.

Other call answering services are available, just Google for one that suits you best.

Local Telephone No's

- Northampton's STD code is 01604
- Wellingborough five miles away is 01933
- Towcester 11 miles away is 01327

I'm sure your own STD codes will be similar in so far that your chosen area may encompass more than one area code. Most people are parochial, meaning they prefer to deal with local companies.

So, we use 'shadow' telephone numbers for example.

Call our

> Towcester Office 01327 123456
> Northampton Office 01604 123789
> Wellingborough Office 01983 456790

All of these numbers can be directed to one phone - **yours!**

You then tap in a code to allow all calls to go to your chosen virtual office. This really does mean you can appear on a par with a *much bigger organisation*, and all whilst working part-time.

Section 6

How to Deal with your Enquiries

As I've stated before, all of your marketing should be making your phone ring. That's the point of your marketing efforts. Shown below is an example of what to say to your prospects when they call you.

Example of how to answer the call from a prospective client

When you receive a call, you need to introduce yourself and have a good opening pitch. You only get one chance to make a first impression, so make sure you practise this beforehand. The more confident you sound, the more credible you will appear.

Ask the Following Qualification Questions to determine Motivation

- ✓ Name
- ✓ Telephone Number
- ✓ What type of property is it?
- ✓ How many bedrooms and other rooms does it have?
- ✓ Does it have a garden?
- ✓ Does it have a garage?
- ✓ Does the property need any work to it?
- ✓ What's the reason you're selling your property?
- ✓ Can you tell me if the property is currently on the market with an estate agent? If so, which agent(s) and how long on the market?

✓ Have you had any estate agents' or independent valuations carried out?

✓ If yes, What is the value?

✓ If no, Do you have an idea of the value?

✓ Have you had any viewings, or any offers?

✓ What would be the ideal outcome for you?

✓ If I agreed to buy your property today, what price would you accept?

✓ Is the property currently facing a repossession order?

✓ Are there any arrears or outstanding mortgage payments?

✓ What is your outstanding mortgage?

✓ Do you have any other debts, with respect to the property, that you need to clear?

✓ When would be a good time or me to pop round and see you to find out if we could work something out that would help you move on...

✓ Would tomorrow at 4.10 suit you or would you prefer Friday at 7.40pm?

Wait for reply...book time and date that you both agree upon. Enter it into your diary and prepare to go!

What to say to your Vendor at your Appointment

Firstly, having made an appointment at a very specific time, i.e. 4.10 or 7.55 **please** ensure you are <u>punctual!!</u> This is really important to give you the upper hand in your negotiations. If you are running more than three minutes late, then phone ahead and let your prospective client know. They will appreciate the gesture.

OK, now go to the front door and knock hard (not meekly) as they open the door, you wipe your feet. This is subliminal and tells them you expect to be let in.

YOU: *"Hello, I'm (your name), good to see you. It's a great place you have here. I really like your (whatever appeals to you or catches your eye).*

Now establish **both parties** will be in attendance. <u>If not re-book</u> or you will just waste your time.

YOU: *"Can I ask why you are selling?"* **(get answers here, their answers are like golden bullets that you use later on)**

Go to the *kitchen* with both parties this is the <u>very best</u> place to get their attention. *(Not the lounge).*

YOU: *"My aim here today is to get some answers to a couple of questions I have, do you mind if I ask them?"*

"How long have you had your house on the market?"

"Have you had any viewings, I bet you've had lots of offers, when are you looking to move?"

"When do you plan on settling in your new place?"

"What will happen if you don't sell?"

"What are you going to do with the leftover (amount of cash)?"

"In your opinion (sellers name here), in this market, what do you realistically expect to get?"

"Which means you'd get how much for yourself?"

"Sounds fair to me, suppose I could match that so you could move on. Is there any reason why you couldn't agree a sale today?"

From this you could determine both motivation and how much mortgage they have.

For example:

They clear £5,000 from a £140,000 house sale = mortgage therefore is £135,000.

Would you then offer £5,000 to get the deal there and then? Or would you ask, *"What is the least you would accept to get a sale this week?"*

Let them answer. Then ask them *"How much Estate Agent Fees would be taken from 'Your bit?'"*.

The answer might surprise you.

In four of my cases, £1.00 was enough to do a deal there and then.

Now clearly, as scripts go this was just a small start but it is enough to get you going!

You will not get every deal!

Get over it!

You will improve

Get used to it!

You can improve

Get more education!

See my manual. This contains much more information, scripts and real life situations to help you move on with your new property business.

You do not need it, but it will give you a flying start and it comes with a 100% Money Back Guarantee!

You really cannot lose. See over for more details.

Section 7

Next Steps,
Action List, The Manual,
Suggested Reading
& Glossary

Next Steps

Here is the crunch. This is where you put the book down and do one of two things,

(1) Do nothing, and then be surprised when nothing happens, except more of the same. Please don't do that. Don't be one of the 95% who go to training days, get confused and do nothing. Don't let this be you!

(2) Promise yourself that tomorrow you will start, or next week, or maybe just after Christmas, or some such nonsense.

Please do something about a brighter tomorrow today!

I will be happy to help, I have a manual that will take you to the next level (read on for details) - after all, I have managed to do it, so why not you? Just take small steps to a bright future of residual income, an income that pays you each month, month in and month out, without your on-going input!

Whatever you decide, I really do wish you well in your future endeavours, and hope to be a part of it.

Good luck.

Regards.

Freddie

F. Rayner.

Action List

Set your goals. Be realistic, ask yourself why are you embarking on this new venture?

Is it because you want a bigger house? Do you want a new or newer top of the range car?

Maybe an exotic holiday would be high on your list of must have's?

This is your chance to create a dream for yourself! So dream away!

It really doesn't matter what you put down on this list, because it is YOUR list. Whatever your motivation, the important thing is to act upon it and believe **YOU CAN DO IT!**

To help you to visualise your goals get a picture of it (or them) and put them on your wallpaper on your computer and on your fridge door and in your bathroom, you get the picture, see it every day and start moving towards getting it. It will happen for you if you take action. OK, so here is your to-do-list to get started.

> ➢ Get yourself a Solicitor who knows about Options, not your high street solicitor who does conveyancing, as these guys are pretty useless.

> ➢ I have made a recommendation at the back of this book with the guys I've actually used, but please feel free to find your own.

> ➢ If you are not a handy person (I'm certainly not) you will need someone who can give you quotes quickly

and acts promptly too. And could be good for leads!

- ➢ Financial Advisor. You will need to contact one should you need a credit report on a potential tenant buyer as a FA will be able to tell you if your tenant buyer will qualify for a mortgage to be able to compete the deal in a few years' time. Also a great source of leads!

- ➢ Order your leaflets

- ➢ Order your stickers

- ➢ Buy some bandit boards

- ➢ Put up an advert in your local paper classified only, not display

- ➢ Put a sign on your car 'We buy Houses' and your telephone number

- ➢ Arrange for your phone to at least have an answer message or get a virtual office

- ➢ Re-read your scripts, OUT LOUD!

- ➢ Start every day by making a to-do list

- ➢ Good Luck! I hope I can be of help to you in the future.

THE MANUAL

HOW YOU TOO CAN BUY HOUSES FOR JUST *ONE POUND!*

Controlling properties with a lease and option is exactly what I have already done and others are doing right now .... often with just ONE POUND.

It really is simple once you have a firm grasp of the buying power using these lease option tactics.

You just leave the existing mortgage in place and take over the payments, then you get in a renter or tenant buyer to make all the payments on your behalf plus a healthy cash flow profit for yourself.

It's fully legal and has been used by experienced investors for many years and now it's your chance to prosper by using my manual.

No credit checks! This works for anyone because you never have to quality for a loan or mortgage! It's already in place! So don't let a poor credit score hold you back!

None of Your Money Invested! Except just one pound! Just learn to deal with very motivated sellers. These people just want out! You are the one doing them a favour!

www.PropertyForAPoundManual.com

Sell On Your Deals For Cash! No money down, no loans, that means you can get property under your control for just one pound, then sell on your assignable deals to other hungry investors for anything from £3,000 - £10,000 each!

I just know that you are really serious about making extra money or even a total career change from property as you've already read this far. So you want to change your life for the better and you really can, IF you just spend a few hours each and every week actioning what my manual teaches you to do in simple steps. That's not too much to ask yourself is it?

You won't have to spend £6,000- £15,000 on a seminar or 'boot camp' and you don't need to spend years studying and learning.

I did it in just one year – and so can you!

My manual makes your learning easy. It is packed with essential information needed to do deals safely and earn you thousands of pounds for each deal whether or not you decide to keep them!

What not to do is also just as important as what you really should do. I've made mistakes so you don't have to. Simple as that and it is guaranteed 100% money back if you do not make money from doing option deals – what could be fairer than that?

I'm on a mission to help you achieve your goals whatever they are. So here is what to do next.

Your investment in your future as a property investor using No Money Down by using lease options will be only £97.00, with **a 100% money back guarantee!!**

Go to www.propertyforapoundmanual.com and place your order today.

P.S. As a bonus, you will also receive the '*Last Property Secret*' report FREE. This will show you how to get land and property for NOTHING using adverse possession techniques. This report really is an eye opener and it is yours for FREE when you invest in my *Property For A Pound Manual.*

www.PropertyForAPoundManual.com

Suggested Reading

Rich Dad, Poor Dad
Robert Kiyosaki

Investing in Real Estate with Lease Options and 'subject to' deals
Wendy Patton

See you at the Top
Zig Ziglar

The Lazy Mans' way to riches
Joe Karbo

Outrageous Advertising
Bill Glazer

The Ultimate Small Business Marketing Book
Dee Blick

(This is the book that helps you understand the A.I.D.A. principle)

Additional resource list

Solicitors MS Law; Contact Paul Gelder tel 0161 772 4500

Printers and suppliers of marketing materials.
Www.property-leaflets.co.uk. Contact Dave Jolley 07768 533078

Glossary

AIDA: An acronym for: Attention, Interest, Desire, Action

Arrears: Overdue debt or rent.

Back End Profit: Back End Profit is the sum of money made at the term end

Bandit Board: Any size made from any suitable material. Home-made looking advert, hand written to look 'cheap' and screams 'bargain' at potential viewers.

BMV Deal: Below market value i.e. purchased for or less than current value

Buy to Let: Referring to the purchase of a property specifically to let out.

Cash Flow: Money made over the mortgage costs from payment made by tenant or tenant buyer.

Equity: The difference between current market value and mortgage owed on property

Full Market Value: Current readily achieved price for property.

Lease: A lease is a contractual arrangement calling for the lessee (user) to pay the lessor (owner) for the use of an asset

Lease Option/or **Lease with an option to purchase:**	This is a contract whereby the property owner and tenant agree that at the end of a specific rental period, the renter has the option, but not the obligation to buy the property at a pre-agreed price.
Option to purchase:	A form of property purchase which combines a rental agreement with the exclusive option of right of first refusal to later purchase the home.
Rent:	Payment for the use of a resource
Rent now, buy later option:	See *Rent to own*.
Rent to Buy:	As rent to own
Rent to Own:	A legally documented transaction under which property is leased in exchange for payment with the option to buy at a pre-determined date.
Tenant:	An occupier of a property.
Tenant Buyer:	A renter with an option to buy with an exclusive right to purchase.